Oxford SPeLLIng

Dr Tessa Daffern

STUDENT BOOK

3

Name:

Class:

OXFORD
UNIVERSITY PRESS
AUSTRALIA & NEW ZEALAND

Oxford University Press is a department of the University of Oxford.
It furthers the University's objective of excellence in research,
scholarship, and education by publishing worldwide. Oxford is a registered
trademark of Oxford University Press in the UK and in certain other
countries.

Published in Australia by
Oxford University Press
Level 8, 737 Bourke Street, Docklands, Victoria 3008, Australia.

First published 2021
Reprinted 2024

ISBN 9780190326111

Reproduction and communication for educational purposes

Edited by Lucy Ridsdale
Cover illustration by Lisa Hunt
Illustrated by Tom Heard
Typeset by Integra Software Services Pvt. Ltd., Pondicherry, India
Proofread by Anita Mullick
Printed in China by Golden Cup Printing Co Ltd

Oxford University Press Australia & New Zealand is committed to sourcing
paper responsibly.

Acknowledgements

A Spin Around the Earth, by Gordon Coutts, illustrated by Dan Crips, Oxford Reading for Comprehension, 2019,
Oxford University Press; *A World of Reptiles* by Nicolas Brasch, Oxford Reading for Comprehension, 2019, Oxford
University Press; *Festival Foods* by Cameron Macintosh, Oxford Reading for Comprehension, 2019, Oxford
University Press; *Stanley Manners* by Joanna Nadin, Oxford Reading for Comprehension, 2019, Oxford University
Press; *Our Siberian Journey* by Bryan Alexander, Oxford Reading for Comprehension, 2019, Oxford University
Press; *Wonders of the World* by Janine Scott, Oxford Reading for Comprehension, 2019, Oxford University
Press; Photographs: Independent Picture Service/Alamy Stock Photo, p. 74; iStock / Getty Images Plus, p. 91;
Shutterstock, pp. 94, 104; Stephanie Jackson – Australian wildlife collection/Alamy Stock Photo, p. 42.

The 'Bringing it together' activities provided online are adapted with permission from Daffern, T. (2018). *The
components of spelling: Instruction and assessment for the linguistic inquirer*. Literacy Education Solutions Pty Limited.

Every effort has been made to trace the original source of copyright material contained in this book. The
publisher will be pleased to hear from copyright holders to rectify any errors or omissions.

WELCOME TO OXFORD SPELLING

Welcome to *Oxford Spelling Student Book 3*! This book contains 28 units that you will use across the year, and that will help you gain new spelling knowledge and skills.

You will notice that each unit is divided into three sections:

- **Phonology (green section)**
- **Orthography (blue section)**
- **Morphology (purple section).**

This has been done to guide you in the types of thinking you might use to answer the questions in each section.

Tip

- **In the phonology sections, think about the sounds you can hear in words.**
- **In the orthography sections, think about the letter patterns that you know.**
- **In the morphology sections, think about the meaning of base words, prefixes and suffixes.**

At the end of each unit, your teacher will work with you on a 'Bringing it together' activity. This is a chance to bring together all the things you are learning about spelling and apply them to new words!

Your teacher, along with the *Oxford Spelling* superheroes, will be giving you lots of helpful information as you work through this book. Look out for the tips in each unit for handy hints on how to answer questions.

Enjoy *Oxford Spelling*, and meet the two superheroes who will help you become super spellers – Rocket Rae and Flying Freya!

Tip

A phoneme is the smallest speech sound you can hear in a word.

The word 'shop' has three phonemes: **/sh/**, **/o/** and **/p/**.

1 Say each word. Listen to the medial short vowel phoneme. Write each word in the correct box.

Tip

A medial vowel is the vowel sound in the middle of a word.

The medial vowel is **/i/** in the word 'king'. It is **/a/** in the word 'catch'.

| shop | nest | stand | stick | lumps | brand | steps | smashed |

| pest | songs | string | missed | wink | luck | that | block |

| ledge | drums | dropped | jumped |

Short /a/ as in 'sack'	Short /e/ as in 'best'	Short /i/ as in 'drip'	Short /o/ as in 'stop'	Short /u/ as in 'stump'

OXFORD UNIVERSITY PRESS

Syllables in words feel like beats. Every syllable has a vowel phoneme. The word 'kitten' has two syllables: *kit-ten*.

A Spin around the Earth
By Gordon Coutts

Astronauts Yaz and Mohammed took their seats in the space shuttle. They were about to blast off into space on a mission to the International Space Station, far above Earth. The space station needed urgent repairs, so Yaz and Mohammed were taking equipment to fix broken solar panels. The astronauts prepared for launch. The rocket's engines fired up and the shuttle rumbled.

A digraph is two letters that represent one speech sound.

In the word 'shop', **sh** is a digraph. Together, these two letters represent the **/sh/** phoneme.

2 Read the text above. Circle the words with one syllable. Underline all of the digraphs you can find in the text.

Then write a word to match each statement below.

- A word with two syllables: _____

- A word with three syllables: _____

- A word with five syllables: _____

- A word with three phonemes: _____

- A word with four phonemes: _____

- A word with five phonemes: _____

3 Look in a book you are reading in class. Find words with a medial short vowel phoneme. Write some of these words in the boxes. Then underline any digraphs you can find in the words.

Short /a/ as in 'sack'	Short /e/ as in 'best'	Short /i/ as in 'drip'	Short /o/ as in 'stop'	Short /u/ as in 'stump'

1 Find the words in the word search.

f	p	j	v	h	y	s	m	j	q
t	t	h	u	m	b	a	l	c	l
q	e	d	x	b	x	s	h	z	a
u	b	c	c	l	i	m	b	h	m
u	a	r	u	n	j	x	r	y	b
u	j	u	k	t	o	m	b	m	i
r	x	m	w	p	y	b	t	n	t
i	l	b	r	a	u	t	u	m	n
w	c	o	m	b	f	y	i	g	n
d	a	m	z	c	o	l	u	m	n

thumb   comb
column   crumb
climb   tomb
autumn
lamb

2 There are many ways to spell the **/m/** phoneme. Say each word. Circle the letter pattern that spells the **/m/** phoneme in each word.

damp   thumb   column   mother   hammer   prism

autumn   lamb   comb   grammar   crumb   common

> **Tip**
>
> A homophone is a word that sounds the same as another word but looks different and has a different meaning.

1 Read these homophones and their meanings:

there	'There' means 'a particular place' (*I went there*), or 'on that matter' (*I agree with you there*).
their	'Their' means 'it belongs to them' (*Their classroom is tidy*).
they're	'They're' is a contraction. It is short for 'they are' (*They're going to catch the bus*).

2 Write the missing homophone in each sentence. You may use a dictionary to help you.

> there   their   they're

a I hope _____ having fun.

b All children were asked to bring _____ hats.

3 Write your own sentences using the homophones in the boxes.

there	
their	
they're	

Now try this unit's 'Bringing it together' activity, which your teacher will give you.

UNIT 2

1 Say these two words: 'pan', 'ring'. Listen to the final phoneme in each word. Where did you place your tongue to say these two phonemes?

Now say the following words. Can you hear the **/n/** phoneme as in 'pan' or the **/ng/** phoneme as in 'ring'? Write each word in the correct box.

worn   lung   song   action   frozen   being

design   ceiling   gnome   Japan   among   sing   hang   train

hungry   sign   gnaw   align   spring   king   mountain   strong

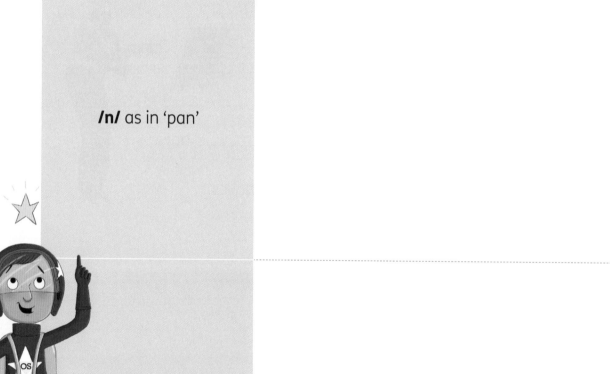

/n/ as in 'pan'

/ng/ as in 'ring'

OXFORD UNIVERSITY PRESS

2 Say each word and count the syllables.

design   spring   ceiling   train

Write each word in the correct box. Then count the phonemes in each word.

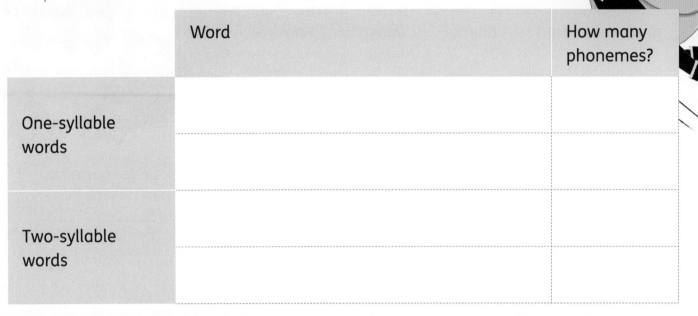

	Word	How many phonemes?
One-syllable words		
Two-syllable words		

1 Write these words in alphabetical order.

nice   gnome   new   knew   country

foreign   animal   sign   knee   banner

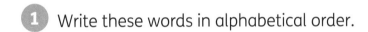

1 _____   2 _____

3 _____   4 _____

5 _____   6 _____

7 _____   8 _____

9 _____   10 _____

2 There are many ways to spell the **/n/** phoneme. Say each word. What letter pattern spells the **/n/** phoneme? Write the missing letter patterns. Write each word in the correct box.

nice   gnome   knot   country   dinner   bonnet

granny   sign   animal   design   knock   knew

numeral   money   minute   gnaw   knee

Letter pattern:	Letter pattern:	Letter pattern:	Letter pattern:
_____	_____	_____	_____

1 Use a dictionary to find out what these homophones mean. Write your definitions in each box. Find the word that has two meanings. Write both definitions of this word.

Morphology

Homophone	Definition
saw	
sore	
soar	

2 Write the missing homophone in each sentence.

saw   sore   soar

a   The birds _____ through the sky.

b   My brother and I _____ a dolphin at the beach.

c   I fell off my skateboard and now my knee is _____.

d   Mum used a _____ to shorten the length of wood.

3 Write your own sentences using the homophones in the boxes.

saw	
sore	
soar	

Now try this unit's 'Bringing it together' activity, which your teacher will give you.

UNIT 3

1 Say each word. Can you hear the **short /a/** phoneme as in 'match' or the **long /a/** phoneme as in 'play'? Write each word in the correct box.

nation   handle   celebrate   rabbit   brain   natural   apple   tape

Short /a/ phoneme as in 'dad'	**Long /a/** phoneme as in 'mate'

2 Look in a book you are reading in class. Find words with the **short /a/** phoneme, and others with the **long /a/** phoneme. Write some of these words in the boxes.

Short /a/ phoneme as in 'catch'	**Long /a/** phoneme as in 'spray'

1 There are many ways to spell the **long /a/** phoneme. Say each word. What letter pattern spells the **long /a/** phoneme? Write each word in the correct box.

brain   trace   nation   vertebrae   plain   weight

reggae   great   clay   survey   locate   stray

favour   eighteen   they   steak

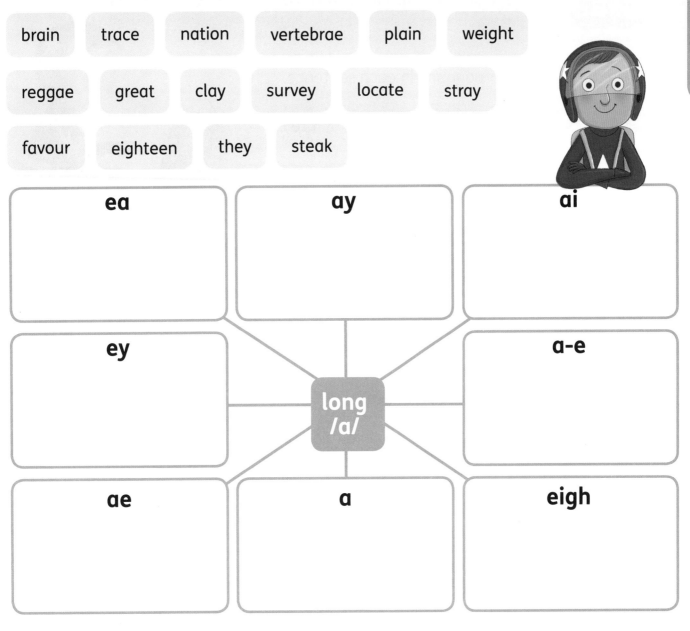

ea	ay	ai

| ey | **long /a/** | a-e |

| ae | a | eigh |

2 Write these words in alphabetical order.

mail   male   prey   pray   weight   wait   great   grate

1 _____   2 _____

3 _____   4 _____

5 _____   6 _____

7 _____   8 _____

It is helpful to use a dictionary when writing homophones.

1 Write the missing homophone in each sentence.

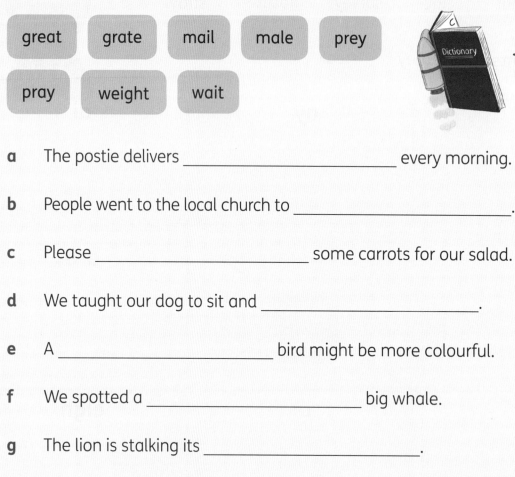

| great | grate | mail | male | prey |

| pray | weight | wait |

a The postie delivers _____ every morning.

b People went to the local church to _____.

c Please _____ some carrots for our salad.

d We taught our dog to sit and _____.

e A _____ bird might be more colourful.

f We spotted a _____ big whale.

g The lion is stalking its _____.

h The cost of the fruit depends on its _____.

2 Choose two homophones from the last activity to write your own sentence.

_____

_____

Now try this unit's 'Bringing it together' activity, which your teacher will give you.

UNIT 4

1 Say each word. Can you hear has the **short /e/** phoneme as in 'jest' or the **long /e/** phoneme as in 'meat'? Write each word in the correct box.

pet   see   settle   electric   generation

seasons   threatened   region   equal

east   west   greet   complete   enter

Short /e/ phoneme as in 'kettle'	**Long /e/** phoneme as in 'feet'

2 Look in a book you are reading in class. Find words with the **short /e/** phoneme, and others with the **long /e/** phoneme. Write some of these words in the boxes.

Short /e/ phoneme	**Long /e/** phoneme

1 There are many ways to spell the **long /e/** phoneme. Say each word. What letter pattern spells the **long /e/** phoneme? Write each word in the correct box.

green   team   emu   athlete   chief   receive   keep

region   thief   delete   protein   these   cream   ceiling

east   speech   equal   sweet   brief   season

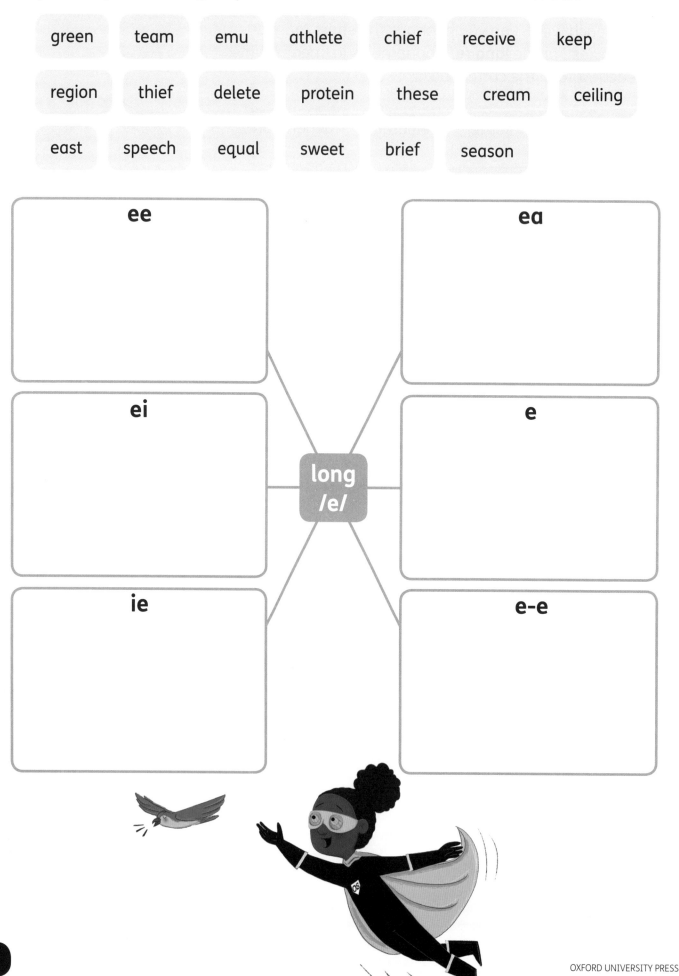

ee

ea

ei

e

long /e/

ie

e-e

> **Tip**
>
> A graph is a letter that represents a speech sound on its own. The letter **b** is a graph in the word 'boy'.
>
> A suffix is a letter or group of letters that go at the end of a base word to make a new word.
>
> 'Meet' (a base word) + **-ing** (a suffix) = 'meeting'

1 Use the rules to complete these sentences using words with the suffix **-ing**. Use the base words provided. Then make up your own sentence using the same rule.

> **If the base word ends with a short vowel graph then a consonant graph, double the last letter and add the suffix -ing.**
>
> drip | dripping   pat | patting   hug | hugging

| drip | Water is _____ from the tap. |
| swim | |

> **Tip**
>
> A trigraph is three letters that represent one phoneme.
>
> In the word 'fetch', **tch** is a trigraph. Together, these three letters represent the phoneme **/ch/**.

> **If the base word ends with x, or with a consonant blend, digraph or trigraph, just add the suffix -ing.**
>
> cast | casting   wash | washing   fetch | fetching

| fetch | The dog is _____ the ball. |
| wish | |

| clean | I am _____ the dirty cupboard. |
| zoom | |

| try | I am _____ to find the lost key. |
| show | |

| whistle | A breeze is _____ outside. |
| joke | |

Now try this unit's 'Bringing
it together' activity, which your
teacher will give you.

UNIT 5

1 Say each word. Can you hear the **short /o/** phoneme as in 'box' or the **long /o/** phoneme as in 'know'? Write the words in the boxes below.

| shopping | throat | problem | hero | wrong | over |

| object | throwing | possible | know | oats |

Short /o/ phoneme as in 'rock'	**Long /o/** phoneme as in 'moat'

2 Look in a book you are reading in class. Find words with the **short /o/** phoneme and the **long /o/** phoneme. Write some words in each box.

Short /o/ phoneme	**Long /o/** phoneme

OXFORD UNIVERSITY PRESS

1 There are many ways to spell the **long /o/** phoneme as in the word 'code'. Say each word. What letter pattern spells the **long /o/** phoneme? Write each word in the correct box.

bureau   although   most   dough   plateau   though   toe

ecosystem   broke   throw   shadow   oats   moat   bone

window   roast   hope   notice   aloe   boat   grow   home

oa	
ow	
o-e	
o	
oe	
ough	
eau	

OXFORD UNIVERSITY PRESS

2 Write these words in alphabetical order, then write a definition for each of them. You may use a dictionary to help you.

| plateau | oats | aloe | moat | bureau |

Word	Definition

Tip

Remember that a suffix is a letter or group of letters that go at the end of a word to make a new word. The suffixes **-s** and **-es** can tell us something is happening now.

1 Use the rules and base words to complete these sentences using words with the suffixes **-s** and **-es**. Then make up your own sentence using the same rule.

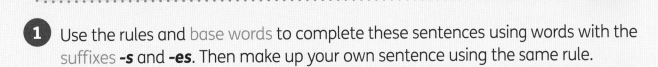

If the base word ends with a consonant graph, blend or digraph, but not s, x, z, ch or sh, add the suffix -s.

drip | drips   rest | rests   laugh | laughs

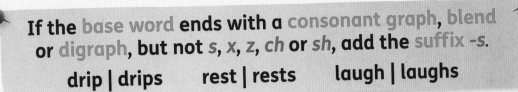

drip	Water _____ from the tap.
hop	

If the base word ends with s, x, z, ch or sh, or a consonant trigraph such as tch, add the suffix -es.

pass | passes   wash | washes   fetch | fetches

fetch	The dog _____ the ball.
stretch	

If the base word ends in a consonant and y, change the y to i and then add the suffix -es.

try | tries   fly | flies   marry | marries

try	The cat _____ to catch the mouse.
carry	

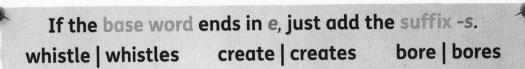

If the base word ends in e, just add the suffix -s.

whistle | whistles   create | creates   bore | bores

whistle	The breeze _____ through the trees.
race	

Now try this unit's 'Bringing it together' activity, which your teacher will give you.

OXFORD UNIVERSITY PRESS

UNIT 6

1 Say each word. Can you hear the **short /oo/** phoneme as in 'book' or the **long /oo/** phoneme as in 'boot'? Write each word in the correct box.

should	through	baboon	stood	rude
threw	wool	football	crooked	June
wooden	good	mushroom	noodles

Short /oo/ phoneme as in 'book'	**Long /oo/** phoneme as in 'boot'

1 There are many ways to spell the **long /oo/** phoneme as in the word 'boot'. Say each word. What letter pattern spells the **long /oo/** phoneme? Circle the letter pattern that represents this phoneme in each word.

blue	flute	broom	soup	crew	through	fruit	juice
youth	grew	June	threw	cute	kangaroo	glue
balloon	true	knew	suit	flew	include

OXFORD UNIVERSITY PRESS

2 Choose three words from the last activity. Write a sentence using each word. Then underline the word with the **long /oo/** phoneme.

a _____

_____

_____

b _____

_____

_____

c _____

_____

_____

Verbs are words for something that happens. 'Talk' is a verb in the sentence, 'I talk to my teacher.'

Tip

Verbs in past tense are words for something that happened in the past. 'Talked' is a past tense verb.

Regular verbs in past tense are spelled using the suffix **-ed**. Sometimes the base verb changes when the suffix is added.

OXFORD UNIVERSITY PRESS

1 Use the rules to complete these sentences using words with the suffix **-ed**. Use the base words provided. Then make up your own sentence using the same rule.

> **If the base word ends with a short vowel graph then a consonant graph other than x, double the last letter and then add the suffix -ed.**
>
> **drop | dropped   skim | skimmed   pat | patted**

drop	I _____ the heavy box.
sip	

> **If the base word ends with x, or with a consonant blend, digraph or trigraph, just add the suffix -ed.**
>
> **camp | camped   crash | crashed   itch | itched**

crash	The waves _____ against the shore.
wish	

> **If the base word has a medial vowel digraph, just add the suffix -ed.**
>
> **float | floated   stain | stained   peel | peeled**

float	The empty bottle _____ on the water.
croak	

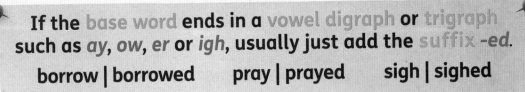

If the base word ends in a vowel digraph or trigraph such as *ay*, *ow*, *er* or *igh*, usually just add the suffix *-ed*.

borrow | borrowed　　**pray | prayed**　　**sigh | sighed**

borrow	We _____ the tub of tennis balls.
follow	

If the base word ends in e, drop the final e and then add the suffix *-ed*.

sprinkle | sprinkled　　**taste | tasted**　　**hike | hiked**

sprinkle	We _____ some water on our pot plants.
cycle	

If the base word ends in a consonant and then *y*, change the *y* to *i* and add the suffix *-ed*.

carry | carried　　**hurry | hurried**　　**vary | varied**

carry	We _____ the shopping bags.
try	

Now try this unit's 'Bringing it together' activity, which your teacher will give you.

OXFORD UNIVERSITY PRESS

UNIT 7

1 Say each word. Can you hear the **short /i/** phoneme
as in 'brittle' or the **long /i/** phoneme as in 'night'?
Write each word in the correct box.

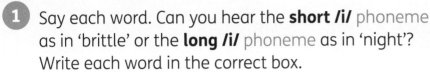

| fright | swim | tie | citizen | multicultural |

| traditional | living | title | invasive | decide |

| mobile | significant | excite | timeline |

Short /i/ phoneme as in 'brittle'	**Long /i/** phoneme as in 'night'

2 Now count the syllables in each word. Write words from the last activity in the
correct box.

Two syllables	
Three syllables	
Four syllables	
Five syllables	

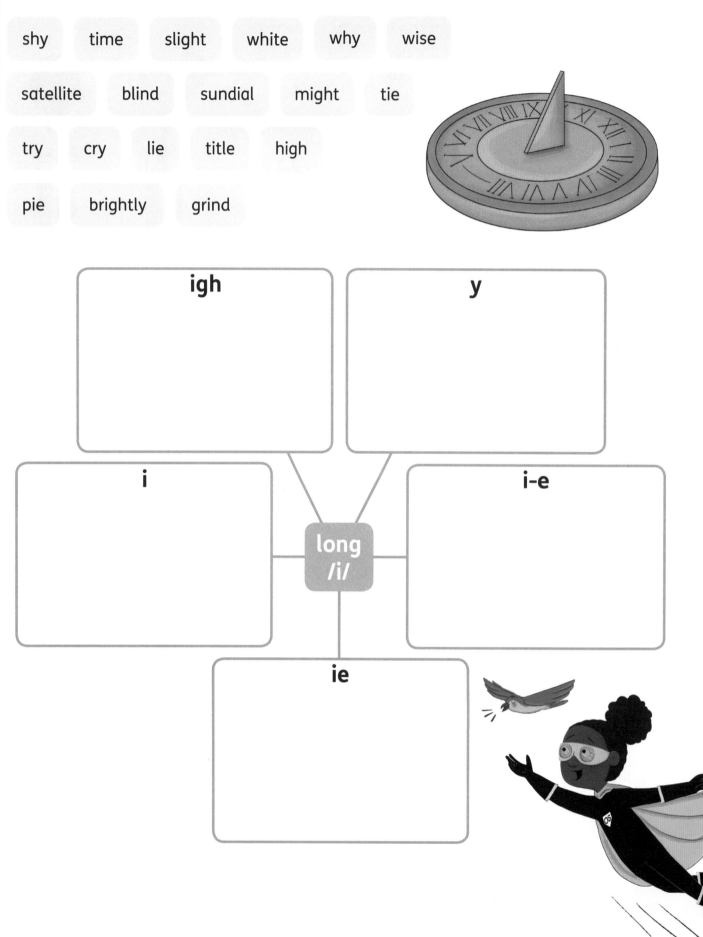

1 There are many ways to spell the **long /i/** phoneme. Say each word. What letter pattern spells the **long /i/** phoneme? Write each word in the correct box.

shy   time   slight   white   why   wise

satellite   blind   sundial   might   tie

try   cry   lie   title   high

pie   brightly   grind

igh

y

i

i-e

long /i/

ie

OXFORD UNIVERSITY PRESS

Tip

A noun is a word that is a name for something.

A plural is a word for more than one thing. The suffixes **-s** or **-es** can be added to many nouns to make plurals.

'Bird' is a noun. 'Birds' is the plural.

1 Use the rules for plurals to complete these sentences.

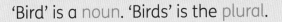

If the base word ends in s, x, z, ch or sh, add the suffix -es.
box | boxes   coach | coaches   flash | flashes

torch | They used all ten _____ inside the cave.

If the base word ends in f or fe, it is usual to change the f or fe to a v and then add the suffix -es.
leaf | leaves   calf | calves   knife | knives

hoof | The horses' _____ made a clopping noise on the road.

If the base word ends in a vowel and the letter o, add the suffix -s.
kangaroo | kangaroos   stereo | stereos   zoo | zoos

zoo | During the holidays, we visited two _____.

If the base word ends in e, just add the suffix -s.

snake | snakes   phone | phones   tree | trees

culture

The festival celebrates many _____.

If the base word ends in a consonant and then o, it is usual to add the suffix -es.

hero | heroes   tomato | tomatoes   echo | echoes

dingo

We went to the zoo to see a pack of _____.

If a base word ends in a consonant and then y, change the y to i and add the suffix -es.

family | families   fly | flies   lolly | lollies

community

The council supports many _____.

Now try this unit's 'Bringing it together' activity, which your teacher will give you.

OXFORD UNIVERSITY PRESS

UNIT 8

Consonant phonemes are either voiced or unvoiced. To make a voiced phoneme, you need to use your voice. Unvoiced phonemes are sounds made using your breath.

The **/zh/** in 'trea<u>s</u>ure' is a voiced phoneme.
Other examples are **/d/**, **/v/**, **/b/**, **/g/** and **/z/**.

The **/sh/** in '<u>sh</u>op' is an unvoiced phoneme.
Other examples are **/t/**, **/f/**, **/p/**, **/k/** and **/s/**.

Tip

1 Say each word. Can you hear the **/sh/** phoneme, which is unvoiced, or the **/zh/** phoneme, which is voiced? Write each word in the correct box.

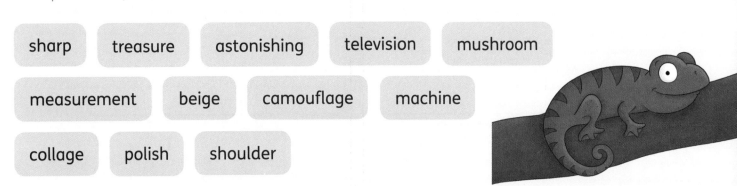

| sharp | treasure | astonishing | television | mushroom |

| measurement | beige | camouflage | machine |

| collage | polish | shoulder |

/sh/ phoneme (unvoiced) as in 'wish'	/zh/ phoneme (voiced) as in 'vision'

2 Count the syllables in the words from the last activity. Write a word in each box.

Two syllables	Three syllables	Four syllables

1. There are many ways to spell the **/sh/** phoneme. Say each word. What letter pattern spells the **/sh/** phoneme? Write each word in the correct box.

shrink   machine   station   magician   tension   chef   motion

fashion   vicious   perish   precious   cushion   brochure   friction

parachute   tradition   pension   special   mansion

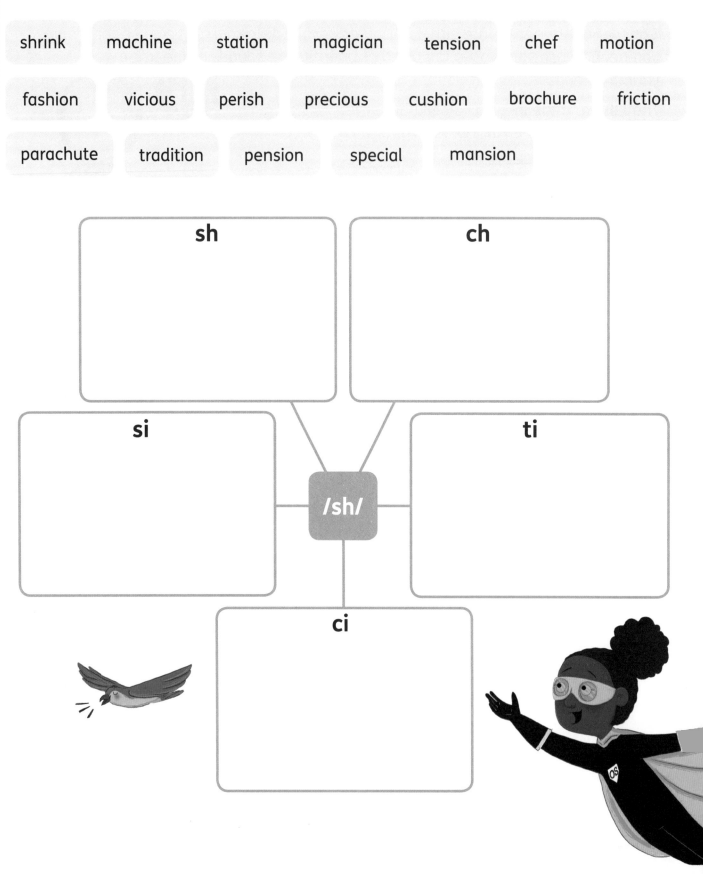

sh	ch

si	ti

/sh/

ci

2 Look at the words in the last activity. Choose three words from this list that you do not write very often. Write a definition for each of these words. You may use a dictionary to help you.

Word	Definition

Tip

The suffix **-ure** can be used to change a verb to a noun.

Morphology

1 Read the rule and examples about the suffix **-ure**. Write two sentences using the nouns given.

> **If the base verb ends in e, drop the e and then add the suffix -ure. If a base verb does not end in e, just add -ure.**

Base word	+ suffix **-ure**	Sentence
please	pleasure	It was a <u>pleasure</u> to meet you.
fail	failure	
depart	departure	

Tip

The suffix **-ion** can also be used to change a verb to a noun.

2 Change each base word to a noun by adding the suffix **-ion**. Read the rule first.

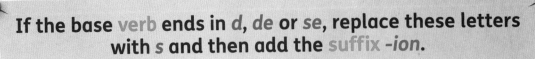

If the base verb ends in *d*, *de* or *se*, replace these letters with *s* and then add the suffix -ion.

Base word	+ suffix *-ion*
comprehend	comprehension
expand	
conclude	conclusion
collide	

Base word	+ suffix *-ion*
revise	
discuss	discussion
express	

3 Choose one of the words you wrote in the last activity. Use it in a sentence.

_____

_____

Now try this unit's 'Bringing it together' activity, which your teacher will give you.

OXFORD UNIVERSITY PRESS

> **Tip**
>
> The onset is the consonant sounds at the beginning of a syllable, and the rime is the vowel and any other sounds that follow.
>
> In the word 'slot', the letters **sl** represent the onset and the letters **ot** represent the rime.

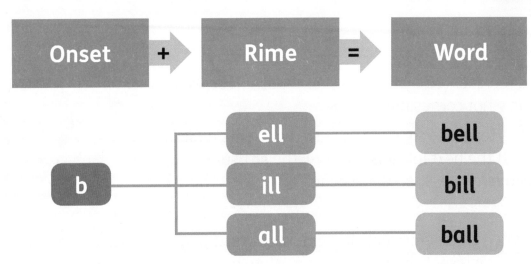

1 Write words in the spaces by adding one of these rimes to the onsets given.

Rimes	**ell** as in 'bell'	**ill** as in 'bill'	**all** as in 'ball' or **awl** as in 'crawl'

f _____   b _____   t _____

c _____   s _____   w _____

y _____   ch _____   sh _____

st _____   dr _____   sm _____

gr _____   sp _____

2 Read the sentences below and on the next page. Some words have a missing rime. Use **ell**, **ill** and **all** to complete the words.

a   **Sh**_____**s** are hard, protective layers formed by some sea creatures.

b   That city has a skyscraper that is the **t**_____**est** building in the world.

c A tennis court is **sm**_____**er** than a soccer field.

d The cat jumped up and **sp**_____**ed** the paint everywhere.

e The winter days are very **ch**_____**y**.

f Sweet and savoury **sm**_____**s** were coming from the chef's kitchen.

The sound represented by the consonant pattern **sc** usually depends on what comes next.

If the next letter is an **r**, **a**, **o** or **u**, the **sc** represents a **/sk/** blend, as in 'scan'. If the next letter is an **e** or **i**, the **sc** usually represents a **/s/** phoneme, as in 'scene'.

Tip

1 Choose three words from activity two on the next page that use different letter patterns to represent the **/s/** phoneme. Write a sentence using each word, and underline the words with the **/s/** phoneme.

a _____

_____

b _____

_____

c _____

_____

Tip

The consonant digraph **ps** at the start of a word represents the **/s/** phoneme. This digraph comes from the Greek language.

OXFORD UNIVERSITY PRESS

2 There are many ways to spell the **/s/** phoneme. Say each word and look at the letter patterns involving the **/s/** phoneme Write each word in the correct box.

loose   circle   scissor   whistle   psychology   straight   certain

decide   voice   increase   cement   worse   assess   sample

bristle   celebrate   address   scene   pseudo   mouse   splendid

scientific   glisten   false   listen   acid   fascinate   psychiatry

fossil   pencil   dust   glass

s	
ss	
se	
ce	
ci	
sc	
st	
ps	

> **Tip**
>
> Adding the suffix **-ment** to the end of a base verb changes the word to a noun.
>
> The meaning of the new word is the result you get from the action of the verb.
>
> For example, if you **measure** something, you get a **measurement**.

1 Read each base verb. Then read each sentence and write the missing noun that matches the base verb, using the suffix **-ment**. One is done for you.

Base word	Sentence
measure	The builder needs an accurate <u>measurement</u>.
achieve	I felt proud of my _____.
entertain	The live _____ was amazing.
equip	Please return the sports _____ to the shed.
develop	There is a new apartment _____ next door.
nourish	Fresh vegetables provide excellent _____.

Now try this unit's 'Bringing it together' activity, which your teacher will give you.

1 Write words using these onsets and rimes.

Onsets	m, w, t, s, b, ch, st		
Rimes	alk, ork or aulk as in 'walk', 'stork' or 'baulk'	ilk as in 'silk'	ulk, as in 'bulk'

Words that end in alk, ork or aulk, as in 'walk', 'stork' or 'baulk'	Words that end in ilk, as in 'silk'	Words that end in ulk, as in 'bulk'

2 Read the sentences. Use **alk**, **ilk** or **ulk** to complete the words with missing letters.

a   S_____**worms** eat mulberry leaves.

b   The cows will be **m**_____**ed** this morning.

c   We **w**_____**ed** all the way to the waterfall.

d   They started **s**_____**ing** when the game was cancelled.

e   I dropped the **b**_____**y** folder and all the paper fell out of it.

blackboard

f   Teachers used to write on a blackboard using a piece of **ch**_____.

1 There are a few ways to spell the **short /e/** phoneme. Say each word. What letter pattern spells the **short /e/** phoneme? Write each word in the correct box.

leg   head   said   feather   stretch   bread   settle

measure   again   spread   hedge   sweat   lettuce

against   method   ready   bellow

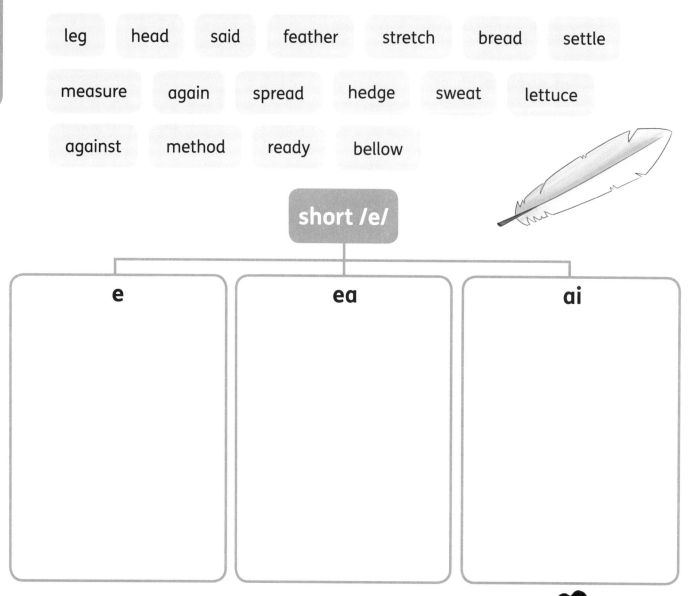

short /e/

e	ea	ai

2 Look in a book you are reading in class. Find words with the **short /e/** phoneme. Write some of the words in the boxes.

Words with **e**	Words with **ea**	Words with **ai**

OXFORD UNIVERSITY PRESS

1 Use the base words to write the missing word in each sentence. Read each sentence to decide which suffix needs to be added to the base word: **-ed** or **-ing**. Use the spelling rules on pages 19–20 and 23–24 to help you.

hop	The rabbit is _____ .
	Yesterday, the rabbit _____ .
thump	My dad is _____ on his drum kit.
	This morning, my dad _____ on his drum kit.
roar	The lion is _____ .
	The lion _____ when it was hungry.
follow	The people are _____ one another.
	The people _____ one another.
scrape	I am _____ the last bit of soup out of the bowl.
	Last night, I _____ the last bit of soup out of the bowl.

Now try this unit's 'Bringing it together' activity, which your teacher will give you.

Phonology

1 Write words using these onsets and rimes.

Onsets	b, f, h, r, j, w, l, br, fr		
Rimes	**udge** as in 'budge'	**idge** as in 'bridge'	**edge** as in 'ledge'

Words that end in **udge**, as in 'budge'	Words that end in **idge**, as in 'bridge'	Words that end in **edge**, as in 'ledge'

2 Read the sentences. Use **udge**, **idge** or **edge** to complete the words with missing letters.

a   The farmland is surrounded by a bushy **h** _____.

b   Three **j** _____**s** will decide who the winner is.

c   The mountain **r** _____ separates two towns.

d   Construction of the **br** _____ took one year.

e   Both of the **fr** _____**s** are full of fresh groceries.

f   Please cut the apple into equal **w** _____**s**.

g   We tried peeling the sticker off, but it wouldn't **b** _____.

h   The grasses grew strangely on the rocky **l** _____.

i   For a treat, we had chocolate **f** _____.

> **Tip**
> To look up a word in the dictionary, start by finding the base word.

1 Choose two words from this list that you do not write very often. Write a definition for each of these words. You may use a dictionary to help you.

| juggle | gigantic | sage | edge | jungle | jumped | magical |

| huge | bridge | stage | enjoy | wedge | engine |

| gentle | justice | image | original | porridge | badge |

Word	Definition

2 Say each word in the list from the last activity. Look at the letter patterns involving the **/j/** phoneme. Write each word in the correct box.

j	
ge	
dge	
gi	

3 Find the words in the word search.

m	h	g	i	g	a	n	t	i	c
a	u	g	i	n	g	e	r	c	g
g	g	e	n	t	l	e	s	n	o
i	e	b	s	e	n	j	o	y	j
c	g	i	r	a	f	f	e	s	u
a	r	a	j	a	r	r	t	t	s
l	r	e	n	g	i	n	e	a	t
o	r	i	g	i	n	a	l	g	i
c	y	q	j	u	g	g	l	e	c
z	a	p	i	m	a	g	e	i	e

juggle   engine
gigantic   gentle
magical   justice
huge   image
stage   original
enjoy   giraffe
ginger

Tip

Remember to think about the spelling of the base word when adding the suffix **-s** or **-es** to make the plural word. Refer to the spelling rules on pages 27–28 if you need a hand.

Morphology

1 Write a sentence using the plural of each base word. Use a dictionary if you aren't sure what some of the words mean.

Base word	Sentence with plural word
fox	
leaf	
wallaroo	

OXFORD UNIVERSITY PRESS

Base word	Sentence with plural word
cube	
volcano	
diary	

2 Write another sentence with some plural words. Then underline the plural words.

_____

_____

_____

Now try this unit's 'Bringing it together' activity, which your teacher will give you.

Tip

Remember that some phonemes are voiced, meaning you use your voice to say them, and some phonemes are unvoiced, meaning you use your breath rather than your voice.

1 Say each word. Can you hear the **/f/** phoneme, which is unvoiced, or the **/v/** phoneme, which is voiced? Write each word in the correct box.

| force | photograph | division | dolphin | environment |

| phenomenon | friction | different | observing | curve |

Words with the **/f/** phoneme	Words with the **/v/** phoneme

2 Look in a book you are reading. Add some more words to the table in the last activity.

OXFORD UNIVERSITY PRESS

3 Say each word and count the syllables.

| phenomenon | force | observing | friction |

Write each word in the correct box. Then count the phonemes.

	Word	How many phonemes?
One-syllable word		
Two-syllable word		
Three-syllable word		
Four-syllable word		

Tip

The letter **v** doesn't go by itself at the end of a word. If a word ends with the **/v/** phoneme that is represented by the letter **v**, it always ends with **ve**, as in the words 'stove' and 'give'.

1 Find the words in the word search.

s	n	a	i	v	e	b	e	l	i	e	v	e	f	s
x	h	i	w	x	a	f	e	s	t	i	v	e	z	i
c	b	r	a	v	e	n	x	b	w	h	a	l	v	e
l	c	a	p	t	i	v	e	o	l	i	v	e	r	v
n	c	v	h	a	v	e	e	z	q	x	j	d	g	e
h	v	f	o	r	g	i	v	e	l	z	z	o	y	q
u	m	r	s	w	e	a	v	e	f	a	w	v	g	n
s	h	o	v	e	d	s	g	l	o	v	e	e	f	j
c	u	x	i	p	f	d	s	a	i	l	v	o	w	k
a	b	f	t	n	l	a	c	t	i	v	e	f	c	h

halve   sieve
have   brave
shove   captive
weave   festive
dove   believe
glove   active
forgive olive

Tip

The **/v/** phoneme is usually represented by the letter **v** and a vowel letter usually comes after it. The word 'of' doesn't follow this rule.

2 Look in a book you are reading. Find words with the **/v/** phoneme, apart from the word 'of'. Write down two of these words and copy the sentences you found them in. Underline the letter **v** and the vowel letter that comes after it.

Word	Sentence

Morphology

Tip

The suffix **-er** can change a base verb into a person noun.

The verb 'teach' changes to the noun 'teacher'. A person who teaches is a teacher.

1 Change each base verb to a person noun by adding the suffix **-er**.

Verb	Noun + suffix **-er**
teach	teacher
climb	
think	
own	

Verb	Noun + suffix **-er**
plumb	
speak	
photograph	

2 Change each base verb into a noun by adding the suffix **-er**. Read the two rules first.

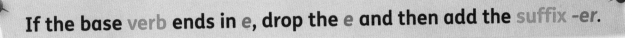

If the base verb ends in e, drop the e and then add the suffix -er.

Verb	Noun + suffix **-er**
bake	baker
drive	
manage	

Verb	Noun + suffix **-er**
ride	
make	
dance	

If the base word ends with a short vowel graph followed by a single consonant graph, double the last letter and add the suffix -er.

Verb	Noun + suffix **-er**
run	runner
swim	
babysit	

Verb	Noun + suffix **-er**
win	
rob	
jog	

Now try this unit's 'Bringing it together' activity, which your teacher will give you.

UNIT 13

Tip

A diphthong is a kind of long vowel sound that you make by moving your mouth in two ways.

/ow/ in the word 'now' and **/oi/** in the word 'toy' are diphthongs.

Even though a diphthong is a changing sound, it counts as one long vowel phoneme and part of one syllable.

1 Say each word. Can you hear the **/ow/** phoneme or the **/oi/** phoneme? Write each word in the correct box.

| voyage | crowd | bounce | coin | proud | mouse | allow |

| round | moisture | annoy | employ | poison | disappoint |

| tower | mountain | loyal | toy | joy | bound | boy | join |

| shower | announce | oyster | frown | sound | soybean | loud |

Words with **/ow/** phoneme	Words with **/oi/** phoneme

OXFORD UNIVERSITY PRESS

2 Say each word and count the syllables.

| disappointed | round | employment | poison |

Write each word in the correct box. Then count the phonemes in each word.

	Word	How many phonemes?
One-syllable word		
Two-syllable word		
Three-syllable word		
Four-syllable word		

1 Read the words listed below and on the next page.

- Circle the **ou** digraph.
- Draw a line under the **ow** digraph.
- For each group of words, describe the letter patterns that are the same in each word. One is done for you.

Word groups	Common letter pattern
now how cow	These words all end in the **ow** digraph.
brown clown frown	
tower power shower	

Word groups	Common letter pattern
mount count discount	
ounce pounce bounce	
house mouse rouse	
loud proud cloud	
found round sound	

Tip

An adjective is a word that tells us what something is like. 'Bright', 'old', and 'lovely' are adjectives.

The suffix **-er** can be added to adjectives to compare things.

1 Change each adjective by adding the suffix -**er**.

hard: <u>harder</u>　　　　quick: _____　　　　slow: _____

2 Use the rules to add the suffix -**er** to make new words.

If the base word ends in e, drop the e and then add the suffix -er.

safe: <u>safer</u>　　　　wide: _____　　　　large: _____

OXFORD UNIVERSITY PRESS

If the base word ends with a short vowel graph then a consonant graph, double the last letter and add the suffix -er.

big: <u>bigger</u>   hot: _____   thin: _____

If the base word ends in a consonant and then _y_, change the _y_ to _i_ and add the suffix -er.

fluffy: <u>fluffier</u>   happy: _____   lucky: _____

3 Write the missing word in each sentence. Remember to add the suffix **-er** to each base word.

great	The speed of a jet is _____ than the speed of a car.
hot	Summer is usually _____ in the north of Australia than it is in the south.
cloudy	The _____ it became, the cooler it got.

Now try this unit's 'Bringing it together' activity, which your teacher will give you.

UNIT 14

Remember that onsets and rimes are sounds. Sometimes, the same rime can be spelled in different ways.

The letter patterns **ought** and **aught** can represent the same sounds. The letter patterns **ite** and **ight** can represent the same sounds too.

Remember that onsets can be spelled in different ways too. The sound **/n/** can sometimes be spelled **kn** and the sound **/r/** can sometimes be spelled **wr**.

Tip

1 Write words using these onsets and rimes.

Onsets	*b*, *s*, *k*, *c*, *m*, *r* or *wr*, *n* or *kn*, *t*, *l*, *f*, *th*, *sl*, *fr*, *br*	
Rimes	*ort*, *ourt*, *aught*, *ought*, *aut* or *orte* as in 'bought' and 'caught'	*ight*, *ite* or *yte* as in 'bright' and 'bite'

Words that end in *ort*, *ourt*, *aught*, *ought*, *aut* or *orte*, as in 'bought' and caught'	Words that end in *ight*, *ite* or *yte*, as in 'bright' and bite'

2 Read the sentences below. Use **ought**, **aught**, **ort**, **ite** or **ight** to complete the words with missing letters.

a   At the bakery this morning, I **b**_____ some freshly baked bread.

b   We felt **fr**_____**ened** during the earthquake.

c   I **t**_____ my younger sister to write her name.

1 Choose three words from the next activity that you do not write very often. Write a definition for each of these words.

Word	Definition

2 There are many ways to spell the phoneme **/aw/** as in the word 'fork'. Say each word. Look at the letter patterns involving **/aw/** phoneme. Write each word in the correct box on the next page.

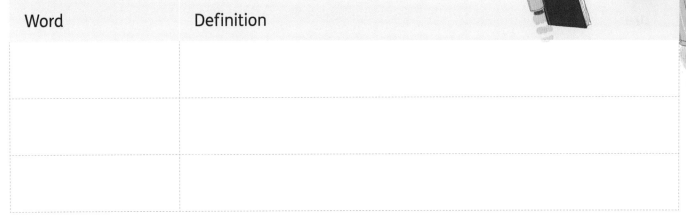

dawn	chalk	soar	snore	four	fought	award	door	small
pour	ignore	astronaut	floor	swarm	normal	bought
author	claw	thought	poor	court	quarter	absorb	wall
board	applaud	talk	carnivore	roar	awful	corner	towards
launch	torch	course	drawn	explore	hoarse

Orthography

or	
aw	
au	
al or *all*	
ar	
oar	
oor	
ore	
our	
ough	

Tip

An adverb is a word that tells us more about what happens.

The suffix **-est** adds the meaning 'most' to base adjectives and adverbs.

1 Change each adjective by adding the suffix **-est**.

hard: <u>hardest</u>   low: _____   high: _____

If the base word ends in e, drop the e and then add the suffix -est.

safe: <u>safest</u>   late: _____   nice: _____

If the base word ends with a short vowel graph then a consonant graph, double the last letter and add the suffix -est.

big: biggest   hot: _____   mad: _____

If the base word ends in a consonant and then y, change the y to i and add the suffix -est.

fluffy: fluffiest   silly: _____   angry: _____

2 Write the missing word in each sentence. Remember to add the suffix **-est** to the base word.

Base word	Sentence
slow	The tired slug moved _____ of all.
hot	The _____ day was Monday.
cloudy	Sunday was the _____ day.

Now try this unit's 'Bringing it together' activity, which your teacher will give you.

Phonology

Tip

In some words, when a vowel is followed by the letter **r**, it can influence the way the vowel sounds. This is called an r-influenced vowel phoneme.

The words 'st**are**', 'b**ir**d' and 'c**ar**t' have an r-influenced vowel phoneme.

1 The words listed below have an r-influenced vowel phoneme. Say each word. Can you hear the **/er/** phoneme as in 'her', the **/air/** phoneme as in 'scare' or the **/ar/** phoneme as in 'dark'? Write each word in the correct box.

Tip

Remember, the word may have a different letter pattern from the example, so listen for the sound it makes.

| mermaid | stark | prepare | mark | third | aware | beware |

| heart | work | square | earth | compare | shark | research |

| disturb | art | harsh |

/er/ as in 'her'	/air/ as in 'scare'	/ar/ as in 'dark'

2 Look in a book you are reading in class. Find words with an r-influenced vowel phoneme. Write some of these words in the boxes below.

/er/ as in 'her'	**/air/** as in 'scare'	**/ar/** as in 'dark'

1 From the list below, choose three words that you do not write very often. Write a definition for each of these words. You may use a dictionary to help you.

thirst   person   Earth   working   journey   thirdly   burn

research   worm   favourite   hurt   mermaid   flavours

worst   learn   first   concern   shirt   term

burst   journal   early   curtain   verb

dirt   worth   word   worship   Perth

Word	Definition

2 There are many ways to spell the **/er/** phoneme. Say each word from the last activity. What letter pattern spells the **/er/** phoneme? Write each word in the correct box.

er	
our	
ir	
or	
ur	
ear	

Tip

Sometimes the **/er/** phoneme can sound a little different, depending on the way a person pronounces it. Sometimes it can sound like a schwa, an **/uh/** sound, but the spelling does not change.

OXFORD UNIVERSITY PRESS

To compare one thing with another, you can use a word ending in a comparative suffix. This is often the suffix **-er**.

> I am **taller** than my little brother.

When you are comparing and want to say what is the **most** something, you can use a word ending in a superlative suffix. This is often the suffix **-est**.

> My big sister is the **tallest** sibling.

Tip

1 Change each base word by adding the suffixes **-er** and **-est**. Use the rules on pages 50 and 51 to help you.

Base word	+ comparative suffix **-er**	+ superlative suffix **-est**
flat		
funny		
safe		
smooth		

2 Use 'hot' as a base word to write the missing words in the sentences. Check if you need to add a suffix.

While the temperature of freshly brewed tea is quite _____,

the temperature of a campfire is _____. However, our sun has

the _____ temperature of the three.

Now try this unit's 'Bringing it together' activity, which your teacher will give you.

1 The words listed below have an r-influenced vowel phoneme. Say each word. Can you hear the **/ear/** phoneme as in 'near', the **/ar/** phoneme as in 'far', the **/air/** phoneme as in 'hair' or the **/er/** phoneme as in 'her'? Write each word in the correct box.

dear   heart   bear   earth   dairy   person   smart

hear   fear   chart   nocturnal   glare   appear   sharpen

research   share

/ear/ as in 'ear'	**/ar/** as in 'far'	**/air/** as in 'air'	**/er/** as in 'her'

2 Look in a book you are reading in class. Find words with an r-influenced vowel phoneme. Write some of these words in the boxes below.

/ear/ as in 'ear'	**/ar/** as in 'far'	**/air/** as in 'air'	**/er/** as in 'her'

1 From the list below, choose three words that you do not write very often. Write a definition for each of these words. You may use a dictionary to help you.

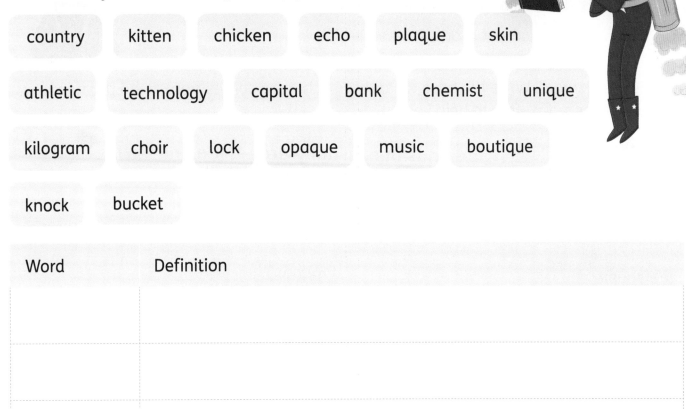

country   kitten   chicken   echo   plaque   skin

athletic   technology   capital   bank   chemist   unique

kilogram   choir   lock   opaque   music   boutique

knock   bucket

Word	Definition

2 There are many ways to spell the **/k/** phoneme. Say each word from the last activity. What letter pattern spells the **/k/** phoneme? Write the word in the correct box.

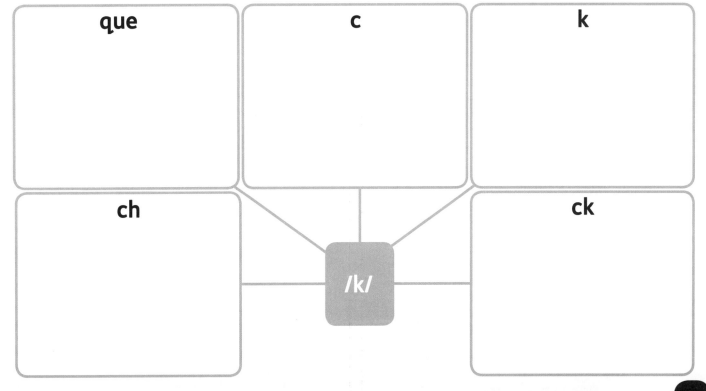

que

c

k

ch

ck

/k/

The suffixes **-able** and **-ible** can be added to some verbs and nouns to make adjectives, which describe what something is like.

The verb 'like' becomes 'likeable'.

The noun 'response' becomes 'responsible'.

 Say each word. Write the base word that each word comes from. Read the rule about the suffix **-ible** to help you.

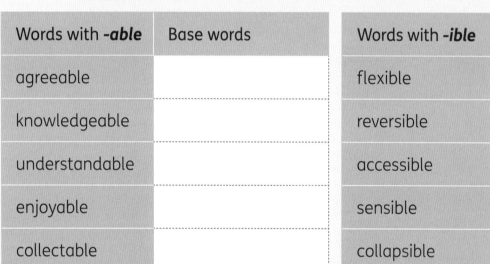

If the base word ends in e, usually drop the e and then add the suffix -ible.

Words with **-able**	Base words	Words with **-ible**	Base words
agreeable		flexible	
knowledgeable		reversible	
understandable		accessible	
enjoyable		sensible	
collectable		collapsible	

2 Write the missing adjectives in each sentence. The words in bold will help you decide what the missing words are. Remember to add the suffixes **-able** or **-ible**.

a It makes **sense** to drink water. It is

_____ to drink water.

b We **enjoy** going to the beach. The beach is an

_____ place to visit.

c I can **reverse** my jacket and wear it inside out. My jacket is

_____.

d My brother and I **collect** stamps. Stamps are a

_____ item.

Now try this unit's 'Bringing it together' activity, which your teacher will give you.

OXFORD UNIVERSITY PRESS

UNIT 17

1 Say each word. Can you hear the **short /a/** phoneme as in 'rattle' or the **long /a/** phoneme as in 'race'? Write each word in the correct box.

| planning | nature | understanding | stage | place | actions |

| matter | contain | rain | calendar | clay | transport |

| maintain | expand | train | mapping | convey | exact |

Short /a/ phoneme as in 'match'	**Long /a/** phoneme as in 'grape'

2 Look in a book you are reading in class. Find five words with the **short /a/** phoneme and five words with the **long /a/** phoneme. Write these words in the boxes below.

Short /a/ phoneme	**Long /a/** phoneme

1 There are many ways to spell the **long /a/** phoneme. Say each word. What letter pattern spells the **long /a/** phoneme? Write the word in the correct box.

fake   trail   nature   Gaelic   steak   grain   eight   vertebrae

prey   break   weight   favour   obey   always   great   danger

Monday   stain   sundae   behave   survey   crayon   male

they   claim   stay   freight   place

ay	
ai	
a-e	
eigh	
a	
ae	
ey	
ea	

OXFORD UNIVERSITY PRESS

2 From the list in the last activity, select three words that you do not write very often. Write a definition for each of these words. You may use a dictionary to help you.

Word	Definition

1 Write the missing homphone in each sentence. You may use a dictionary to help you.

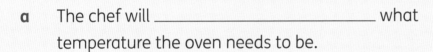

no   know   not   knot

a The chef will _____ what temperature the oven needs to be.

b I had trouble undoing the _____ in my shoelace.

c By the time it got dark, there were _____ kids outside.

d The shrub may _____ survive unless it is watered.

2 Write your own sentences using the homophones in the boxes.

know	
knot	

Now try this unit's 'Bringing it together' activity, which your teacher will give you.

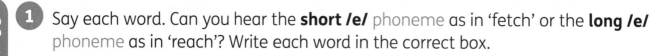

Phonology

1 Say each word. Can you hear the **short /e/** phoneme as in 'fetch' or the **long /e/** phoneme as in 'reach'? Write each word in the correct box.

pest   seed   settlement   seasonal   electrician

enter   eastern   western   greeting   completion

regional   generation   threatening   equally   develop   sea

Short /e/ phoneme as in 'belt'	Long /e/ phoneme as in 'greet'

2 Look in a book you are reading in class. Find words with the **short /e/** phoneme and words with the **long /e/** phoneme. Write these words in the boxes below.

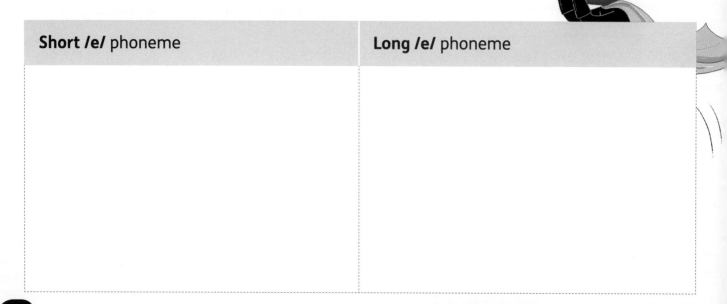

Short /e/ phoneme	Long /e/ phoneme

1 There are many ways to spell the **long /e/** phoneme. Say each word. What letter pattern spells the **long /e/** phoneme? Write the word in the correct box.

speed	beast	medium	concrete	believe	seize	relief

deceive	female	complete	teach	refugee	corroboree

clean	geometric	niece	receive	sleeve	beach	theme

ee	
ei	
ea	
ie	
e	
e-e	

2 From the list in the last activity, select three words that you do not write very often. Write a definition for each of these words. You may use a dictionary to help you.

Word	Definition

Tip

The suffix **-ian** is used to make nouns describing a person.

1 Read each sentence. Underline the word that contains the **-ian** suffix. Then circle the matching base word.

a A person who works with electricity is an electrician.

b A person who works in a library is a librarian.

c A person who performs comedy is a comedian.

d A person who plays music is a musician.

e A person who is from Italy is an Italian.

Tip

The suffix **-ion** is used to turn some verbs into nouns. For example,

The verb 'instruct' becomes the noun 'instruction'.

The verb 'decorate' becomes the noun 'decoration'.

2 Read each sentence. Write the missing verb in each sentence. Use the noun ending in the **-ion** suffix to help you work out what each verb is.

a The zookeepers will _____
the animals. The animals need **protection** because their habitat was lost.

b My brother and I _____
stamps. We have been adding to our **collection** for two years.

c We must _____ quickly.
Quick **action** is needed.

3 Look again at the words ending in the suffix **-ion** from the last activity ('protection,' 'collection' and 'action'). Write a descriptive sentence for each word.

a _____

_____

b _____

_____

c _____

_____

Now try this unit's 'Bringing it together' activity, which your teacher will give you.

1. Say each word. Can you hear the **short /o/** phoneme as 'cost' or the **long /o/** phoneme as in 'blow'? Write each word the correct box.

logical   custodian   motion   responsible

democracy   rotation   offspring   owner

expose   phenomena   conservation   compose

Short /o/ phoneme as in 'off'	**Long /o/** phoneme as in 'boat'

2. Look in a book you are reading. Find some more words to add to the table above.

Tip

Remember that the letter **x** often represents a blend of the phonemes **/k/** and **/s/**.

Say each word and count the syllables.

| custodian | expose | logical | responsible | compose | rotation |

Write each word in the correct box. Count the phonemes.

	Word	How many phonemes?
Two-syllable words		
Three-syllable words		
Four-syllable words		

1 From the list in the next activity, select three words that you do not write very often. Write a definition for each of these words. You may use a dictionary to help you.

Word	Definition

Orthography

2 There are many ways to spell the **long /o/** phoneme as in the word 'boat'. Say each word. What letter pattern spells the **long /o/** phoneme? Write the word in the correct box.

throat   yellow   compose   echo   dough   plateau   toe

though   phone   wrote   toast   follow   float   pillow   host

coast   although   bureau   aloe   elbow   expose   aroma

oa	
ow	
o-e	
o	
oe	
ough	
eau	

OXFORD UNIVERSITY PRESS

3 Find the words in the word search.

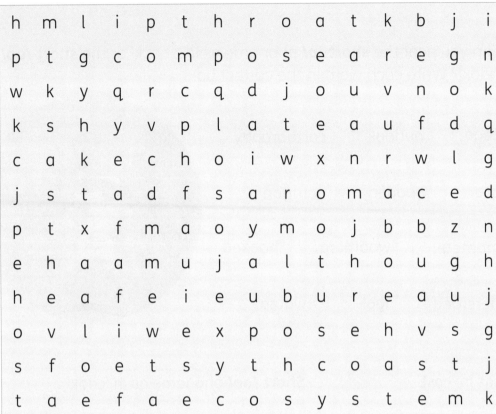

h	m	l	i	p	t	h	r	o	a	t	k	b	j	i
p	t	g	c	o	m	p	o	s	e	a	r	e	g	n
w	k	y	q	r	c	q	d	j	o	u	v	n	o	k
k	s	h	y	v	p	l	a	t	e	a	u	f	d	q
c	a	k	e	c	h	o	i	w	x	n	r	w	l	g
j	s	t	a	d	f	s	a	r	o	m	a	c	e	d
p	t	x	f	m	a	o	y	m	o	j	b	b	z	n
e	h	a	a	m	u	j	a	l	t	h	o	u	g	h
h	e	a	f	e	i	e	u	b	u	r	e	a	u	j
o	v	l	i	w	e	x	p	o	s	e	h	v	s	g
s	f	o	e	t	s	y	t	h	c	o	a	s	t	j
t	a	e	f	a	e	c	o	s	y	s	t	e	m	k

throat
compose
echo
ecosystem
plateau
although
host
coast
bureau
aloe
expose
aroma

1 Write the missing homophone in each sentence. You may use a dictionary to help you.

buy	by	bye	for	four	fore

a It is uncommon to send letters _____ post these days.

b The scientists worked _____ more than a year.

c Environmental issues have recently come to the _____.

d As the bus departed, my friend waved and said '_____'.

e To make the pie, I will need to _____ fresh vegetables.

f The temperature only reached _____ degrees Celsius.

Now try this unit's 'Bringing it together' activity, which your teacher will give you.

1 Say each word. Can you hear the **short /o/** phoneme as in 'shock' or the **short /oo/** phoneme as in 'book'? Write each word in the correct box.

horizontal　footage　outlook　cartography

soot　denominator　wooden　octagon

rhombus　thermometer　woomera　hooked

geography　understood　look　watch

Short /o/ phoneme as in 'cost'	**Short /oo/** phoneme as in 'cook'

2 Look in a book you are reading. Add some more words to the table above.

3 Say each word and count the syllables.

woomera   rhombus   cartography

footage   horizontal   octagon

Write each word in the correct box. Count the phonemes.

	Word	How many phonemes?
Two-syllable words		
Three-syllable words		
Four-syllable words		

1 From the words listed in the next activity, select three words that you do not write very often. Write a definition for each of these words. You may use a dictionary to help you.

Word	Definition

2 There are many ways to spell the **long /oo/** phoneme as in the word 'boot'. Say each word. What letter pattern spells the **long /oo/** phoneme? Write each word in the correct box.

blue   flute   soup   through   glue   true   juice   balloon

knew   suit   bloom   cartoon   new   youth   include

bruise   breakthrough   pollute   coupon   chewing

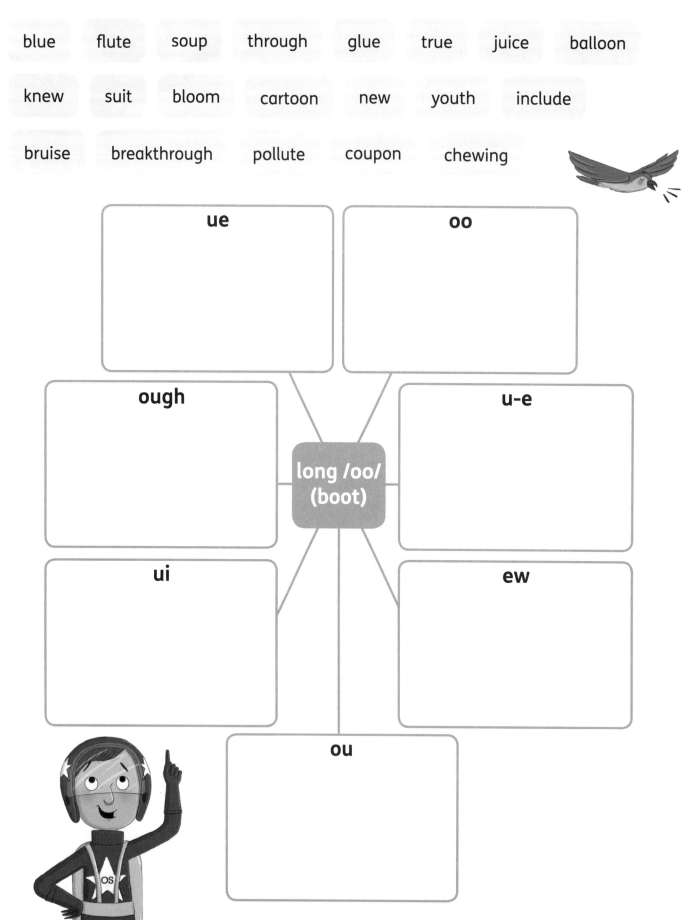

ue

oo

ough

u-e

long /oo/
(boot)

ui

ew

ou

OXFORD UNIVERSITY PRESS

1 Write the missing homophone in each sentence. You may use a dictionary to help you

| weather | whether | horse | hoarse | through | threw |

a Walking _____ the cave was amazing.

b I caught a cold and now my voice is _____.

c We were deciding _____ to celebrate at the park or at home.

d The _____ forecast for the east coast is rainy this week.

e I caught the ball that my teammate _____ to me.

f My friend lives on a farm and enjoys riding his _____.

2 Write your own sentences using the homophones in the boxes.

weather	
hoarse	
through	

Now try this unit's 'Bringing it together' activity, which your teacher will give you.

1 From the list below, choose two words that you do not write very often. Write a definition for each of these words. You may use a dictionary to help you.

multicultural   satellite   traditional   science   prediction   excitement

title   invasive   decide   mineral   fertile   vertical

Word	Definition

2 Say each word from the last activity. Can you hear the **short /i/** phoneme as in 'kit' or the **long /i/** phoneme as in 'kite'? Write each word in the correct box.

Short /i/ phoneme as in 'rich'	**Long /i/** phoneme as in 'ripe'

3 Say each word and count the syllables.

| prediction | science | traditional |

Write each word in the correct box. Then count the phonemes in each word.

	Word	How many phonemes?
Two-syllable word		
Three-syllable word		
Four-syllable word		

1 From the list in the next activity, choose three words that you do not write very often. Write a definition for each of these words. You may use a dictionary to help you.

Word	Definition

2 There are many ways to spell the **long /i/** phoneme. Say each word. What letter pattern spells the **long /i/** phoneme? Write each word in the correct box.

enlighten   classify   satellite   magpie   biography   advice

feisty   supply   highlight   sly   combine   die   climate

slight   kaleidoscope   library   lie

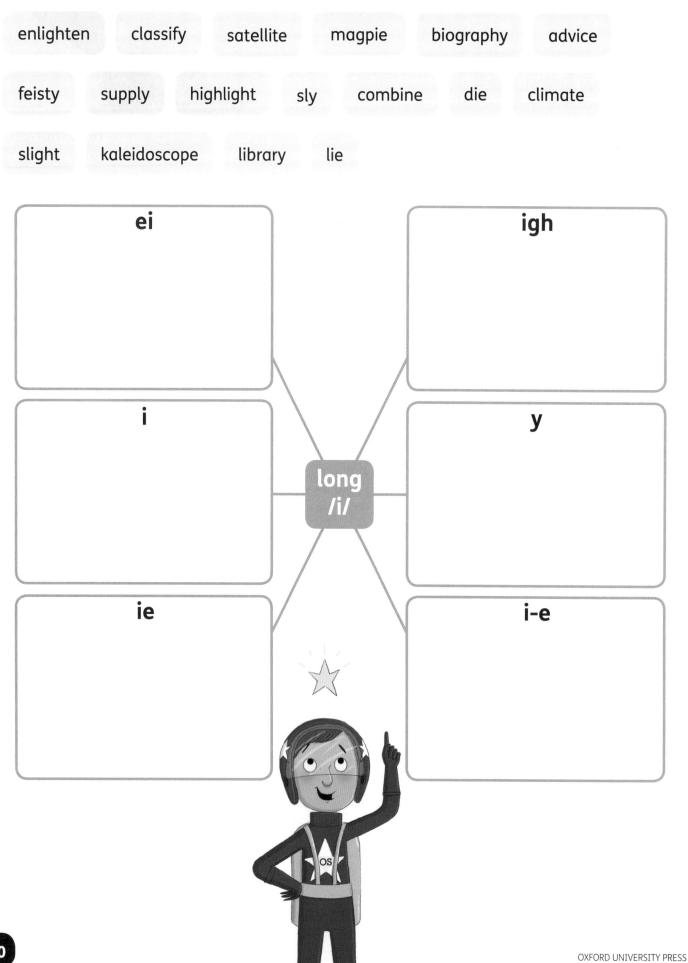

ei

igh

i

y

long
/i/

ie

i-e

The suffix **-ful** can be added to some nouns to form adjectives. This suffix means 'full of something'.

1 Change each base word by adding the suffix **-ful**. One is done for you.

Base word	+ suffix *-ful*	Base word	+ suffix *-ful*
help	helpful	use	
care		doubt	
hope		cheer	
colour		respect	

2 Choose two words with suffixes that you wrote in the last activity. Write a descriptive sentence using these words.

_____

_____

Now try this unit's 'Bringing it together' activity, which your teacher will give you.

Phonology

1 Write words using these onsets and rimes.

Rimes	*ice* as in 'nice'	*ace* as in 'race'	*eece, eace, ease* or *iece* as in 'fleece', 'peace', 'grease' or 'niece'

d_____   r_____   gr_____

f_____   p_____   pr_____

l_____   tw_____   sl_____

m_____   tr_____   sp_____

n_____   br_____   pl_____

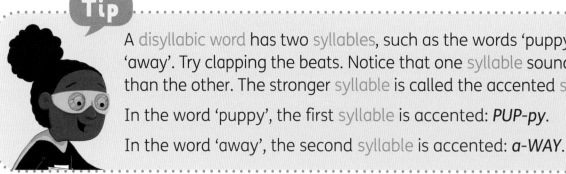

Tip

A disyllabic word has two syllables, such as the words 'puppy' and 'away'. Try clapping the beats. Notice that one syllable sounds stronger than the other. The stronger syllable is called the accented syllable.

In the word 'puppy', the first syllable is accented: *PUP-py*.

In the word 'away', the second syllable is accented: *a-WAY*.

2 Say each word and clap the two syllables. Is the accent on the first or the second syllable? Circle the words with an accented first syllable.

bottle	fastest	below	ripple	remind	castle	away

teaching	mistake	parrot	relieve	silent	behave	receive

jungle	prefer	throttle	escape	challenge	before

Tip

Remember that each syllable has a vowel phoneme. The vowel phoneme in an unaccented syllable is often a schwa. A schwa is an **/uh/** sound.

The words 'jungle' and 'medal' have a schwa in their last syllable.

1 Say each word. Can you hear the schwa before the **/l/** in the last syllable? Look at the letter pattern at the end of the word. Write each word in the correct box below.

| people | animal | ripple | dial | pedal | sample | jungle |

| moral | castle | actual | trial | apple | little | spiral |

Words ending in *le*	Words ending in *al*

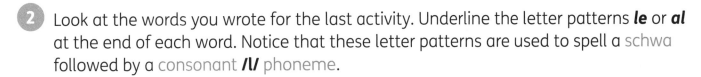

Notice that the word 'animal' has two schwas (in the second and third syllables).

2 Look at the words you wrote for the last activity. Underline the letter patterns **le** or **al** at the end of each word. Notice that these letter patterns are used to spell a schwa followed by a consonant **/l/** phoneme.

3 Look in a book you are reading. Find some more words that end with a schwa followed by a consonant **/l/** phoneme. Write some of these words in the table above.

An adjective is a word that describes something. 'Funny' is an adjective. The suffix **-y** can be used to create an adjective.

An adverb is a word that gives more information about a verb. 'Slowly' is an adverb. The suffix **-ly** can be used to create an adverb.

1 Read the rules and examples to write the missing words.

If a base word ends in a short vowel graph then a consonant graph, it is usual to double the last letter and add the suffix -y to make an adjective.

Base word	Word + suffix **-y**
fun	funny
sun	
fog	

In most cases, if the base word ends in e, drop the e and then add the suffix -y to make an adjective.

Base word ending in **e**	Word + suffix **-y**
ease	easy
laze	
taste	

If a word ends with the suffix -y, change the y to i and then add the suffix -ly to make an adverb.

Word ending in **-y**	Word + suffix **-ly**
easy	easily
lazy	
greedy	

2 Read each word below and then write the base word beside it.

safely		squeaky	
loudly		bravely	
slowly		smelly	
greedy		sleepy	
easy		wildly	

3 Use these words to make up your own sentences. One is done for you.

slowly	I started climbing <u>slowly</u> up the rope.
smelly	
funny	
heavily	
busily	

Now try
this unit's 'Bringing
it together' activity,
which your teacher
will give you.

Phonology

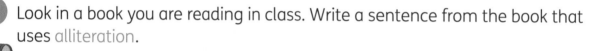

Tip Alliteration is when a group of words all start with the same sound. Find alliteration by listening for a repeating consonant phoneme.

Sometimes alliteration can include a few little words such as 'and' and 'of' that don't match the pattern of repeating consonant phonemes. This is still called alliteration.

The **b**ig **b**lack **b**ugs are **b**ouncing

1 Look in a book you are reading in class. Write a sentence from the book that uses alliteration.

_____

_____

_____

2 Say each word and count the syllables.

| quaintly | quit | quantity |

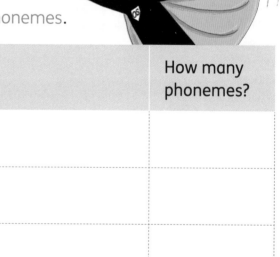

Write each word in the correct box. Count the phonemes.

	Word	How many phonemes?
One-syllable word		
Two-syllable word		
Three-syllable word		

3 Write a sentence that shows alliteration using any of these words. You may add suffixes to the words if you need to.

queen	quaint	quick	queer	quest	quoll	quit

quantity	quite	quiet	quiver	quarrel	question

_____

_____

1 Say each word. Look at the letter patterns that end the last syllable of each word. Notice that each word ends in **or**, **our**, **er** or **ar**. Circle the letter pattern at the end of each word.

doctor	favour	chapter	collar	polar

pillar	error	savour	alter	factor	neighbour	ladder

motor	dollar	flavour	mirror	better	nectar	harbour

humour	author	grammar	bitter	colour	donor	butter

solar	danger	odour	manner	minor

2 Select some words from the last activity to complete the table below and on the next page. Write a sentence using each word. You may use a dictionary to help you.

Word ending	Sentence
or	
our	

Word ending	Sentence
er	
ar	

Tip

Tense shows whether something happened in the past, is happening in the present or will happen in future.

The suffixes **-s** and **-es**, and **-ing**, can tell us about when something is happening.

The suffix **-ed** can be used for past tense, to show that something happened in the past.

Morphology

1 Change each of these base words by adding suffixes that show tense: **-s** or **-es**, **-ing** and **-ed**. Remember to use the rules that you learned earlier. One is done for you.

Base word	+ suffix **-s** or **-es**	+ suffix **-ing**	+ suffix **-ed**
sip	sips	sipping	sipped
watch			
end			
carry			
whistle			

2 Now choose one of these words with a suffix and write a sentence.

_____

_____

Now try this unit's 'Bringing it together' activity, which your teacher will give you.

OXFORD UNIVERSITY PRESS

UNIT 24

> A consonant blend is two or more consonant sounds that join together in a word.
>
> **/str/** is a consonant blend in the word 'string'.
>
> **/shr/** in the word 'shrimp' is a blend of the phonemes **/sh/** and **/r/**.

Tip

1 Say each word. Listen for the consonant blend at the start. In the boxes below, write the different consonant blends at the top, and then the words with that blend.

shrinkable   scratches   stranded   spray   scribe   scroll

stripe   shrill   shred   stretch   strong   shrug

scrape   sprout   sprinkled   spreading

Blend /_____/	Blend /_____/	Blend /_____/	Blend /_____/

2 Look in a book you are reading. Write some more words starting with these consonant blends into the table above.

Festival Foods
by Cameron Macintosh

Food plays a very important role in festivals and celebrations around the world. Many festivals are hard to imagine without the special foods that are a part of them.

3 Read the text above. Write a word in each box below. Then count the phonemes in each word.

	Word	How many phonemes?
One-syllable word		
Two-syllable word		
Three-syllable word		
Four syllable word		

Tip

Have a look at the word 'rabbit'. Many disyllabic words follow this pattern. The first syllable has a short vowel graph: **a**, which represents the **short /a/**. The middle consonant, **b**, is doubled.

The **bb** in 'rabbit' is called a medial consonant doublet.

1 Write the missing consonant letter in these disyllabic words. Say each word and clap the syllables. Circle the letter that represents the short vowel phoneme in the first syllable. One is done for you.

r(a)bbit   mam____al   mid____le   bot____le

hap____y   gig____le   pil____ow   man____er

OXFORD UNIVERSITY PRESS

2 Find words with a medial consonant doublet in the two texts below. Write them into the tables. Use the examples to help you.

Stanley Manners

By Joanna Nadin

Stanley Manners told lies. Not just little white lies, but big, beastly whoppers.

-nn- as in 'banner'	**-tt-** as in 'bottle'	**-pp-** as in 'happy'

Our Siberian Journey

By Bryan Alexander

By the end of August, I noticed a chill in the air – summer was almost over. The tundra looked beautiful with autumn colours of red, yellow and brown.

-mm- as in 'mammal'	**-ll-** as in 'pillow'

1 Write a sentence for each word below. Then underline the suffix **-ian** in each sentence.

electrician	
librarian	
musician	
comedian	
historian	

Tip

Remember to drop the letter **e** at the end of a base verb before adding the suffix **-ion**.

2 Change each verb to a noun by adding the suffix **-ion**. Then write a sentence for each and underline the noun with the suffix **-ion**. One is done for you.

act	action	I like movies with exciting <u>action</u>.
react		
collect		
pollute		

Now try this unit's 'Bringing it together' activity, which your teacher will give you.

OXFORD UNIVERSITY PRESS

1 Write words using these onsets and rimes.

Onsets	b, c, m, g, r or wr, s, h, p, fl, sl, thr, gl, sc, qu	
Rimes	oat or ote as in 'moat' and 'wrote'	oap or ope as in 'soap' and 'hope'

Words that end in **oat** or **ote**, as in 'moat' and 'wrote'	Words that end in **oap** or **ope**, as in 'soap' and 'hope'

2 Use **oat**, **ote**, **oap** or **ope** to complete the sentences.

a I **h** _____ it will be sunny tomorrow.

b This **s** _____ smells like flowers.

c My dog's **c** _____ is long and shiny.

d The castle has a deep **m** _____ all around it.

e I like to collect funny **qu** _____**s** from books I am reading.

A World of Reptiles

By Nicolas Brasch

newt

snake

turtle

crocodile

The most common types of reptiles are:
- amphibians (includes frogs, toads, newts and salamanders)
- crocodilia (includes crocodiles and alligators)
- squamates (includes snakes, lizards and worm lizards)
- turtles (includes turtles, terrapins and tortoises).

3 Choose words from the text above to complete the table. Then count the phonemes in each word.

	Word	How many phonemes?
Two-syllable word		
Three-syllable word		
Four-syllable word		
Five syllable word		

OXFORD UNIVERSITY PRESS

1 There are different ways to write the **/oi/** diphthong as in 'boy'. Say each word. What letter pattern spells the **/oi/** diphthong? In the boxes below, write the different digraphs that spell **/oi/** and the words with that digraph.

Tip

Remember to use your dictionary if you're not sure what a word means.

| point | voice | deploy | coin | boy | annoy | boil | enjoy |

| avoid | royal | foil | joy | moisture | destroy | soil | voyage |

| asteroid | convoy | soybean | choice | employ | ointment | oily |

Digraph: _____

Digraph: _____

1 Write the missing homophone in each sentence. One of the words has two meanings so it belongs in two of the sentences. You may use a dictionary to help you.

| break | brake | bear | bare |

a We walked along the beach in _____ feet.

b The teapot might _____ because it is old and fragile.

c I can't _____ to hear the dogs barking any longer.

d When I slow down using my bike's _____, it makes a squeaking noise.

e The giant panda is a species of _____ that lives in China.

2 Write your own sentences using the homophones in the boxes.

break	
brake	
bear	
bare	

Now try this unit's 'Bringing it together' activity, which your teacher will give you.

1 Write a sentence that shows alliteration using any of these words. You may add suffixes to the words if you need to.

| faint | feather | fly | family | force | friction |

| phenomena | forward | fresh | phone | flip |

| photo | flush | from | fifty | farm | further |

_____

_____

_____

2 Write a word from the list that matches each box below. Then count the phonemes in each word.

	Word	How many phonemes?
One-syllable word		
Two-syllable word		
Three-syllable word		
Four syllable word		

1 There are different ways to spell the **/f/** phoneme. Say each word. What letter pattern spells the **/f/** phoneme? Write each word in the correct box.

feather   photo   fabulous   laugh   effort   digraph   chef

differ   morphology   cough   safely   sniff   forceful   tough

elephant   offer   emphasis   enough   freshest   muffin

philosophy   friction   trough   coffee   phoneme

f	
ff	
ph	
gh	

2 Write a definition for the following words. You may use a dictionary to help you. Then underline all of the letter patterns that represent the **/f/** phoneme.

phonology	
orthography	

OXFORD UNIVERSITY PRESS

morphology	
phoneme	
digraph	

Some verbs are called 'irregular'. Irregular verbs don't use the suffix **-ed** for past tense.

'Am,' 'have,' and 'go' are irregular verbs.

Tip

1 Read these past tense irregular verbs.

won	took	sat	gave	fell	bought	rode	felt

had	told	found	could	thought	built	ran

Write each past tense irregular verb next to its matching present tense word below.

run _____   ride _____   think _____

win _____   buy _____   feel _____

sit _____   tell _____   give _____

can _____   fall _____   build _____

take _____   find _____   have _____

2 Choose three of these irregular verbs and write a past tense sentence for each. Underline the irregular verb in each sentence.

a _____

_____

b _____

_____

c _____

_____

Now try this unit's 'Bringing it together' activity, which your teacher will give you.

1 Write a sentence that shows alliteration using any of these words. You may add suffixes to the words if you need to.

| throw | thing | thirteen | thumb | thread | third | thigh |

| thief | thank | thump | Thursday | theatre | thoughtfully |

| thirsty | theatrical | thousand | thermometer |

_____

_____

_____

2 Write some words from the last activity in the boxes below. Then count the phonemes in each word.

	Word	How many phonemes?
One-syllable word		
Two-syllable word		
Three-syllable word		
Four syllable word		

1 There are different ways to spell the **/g/** phoneme as in 'go'. Say each word. What letter patterns spell the **/g/** phoneme? Write each word in the correct box.

gherkin   plague   guess   yoghurt   haggle   demographic

analogue   juggle   dragon   vague   kilogram   Afghan

wiggle   dinghy   hexagon   guitar   guard

g	
gue	
gg	
gh	
gu	

2 Write a definition of each word below. You may use a dictionary to help you. Then underline all of the letter patterns that represent the **/g/** phoneme.

hexagon	
analogue	
demographic	
dinghy	

OXFORD UNIVERSITY PRESS

A prefix is a letter or group of letters that go at the start of a base word to make a new word.

The prefix **un-** changes the base word 'happy' into a new word: 'unhappy'.

Tip

1 Use these charts to help you make words that start with the prefixes **mis-** and **dis-**. Add a prefix and a suffix to each base word and write your words in the boxes below. Note, not all suffixes will make words with each base word.

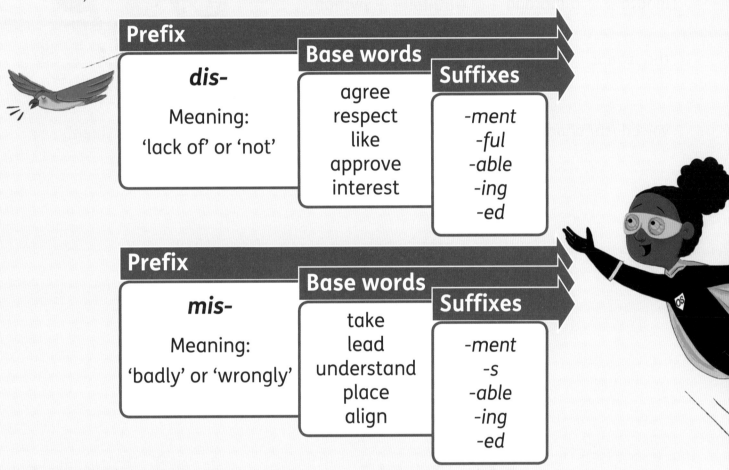

Prefix

dis-

Meaning: 'lack of' or 'not'

Base words

agree
respect
like
approve
interest

Suffixes

-ment
-ful
-able
-ing
-ed

Prefix

mis-

Meaning: 'badly' or 'wrongly'

Base words

take
lead
understand
place
align

Suffixes

-ment
-s
-able
-ing
-ed

Words + prefix **dis-**	Words + prefix **mis-**

Now try this unit's 'Bringing it together' activity, which your teacher will give you.

UNIT 28

1 Say each word. Can you hear the voiced **/th/** phoneme or the unvoiced **/th/** phoneme? Write each word in the correct box.

| altogether | mathematics | feather | gather |

| length | marathon | truthful | python |

| thousands | another | therefore | although |

voiced **/th/** phoneme as in 'the'	unvoiced **/th/** phoneme as in 'three'

Wonders of the World

By Janine Scott

There are beautiful World Heritage sites all around the world. Some countries, such as Italy and China, have more than 50 World Heritage sites. Other countries have only one site. Each site is unique and special, allowing people to experience something they cannot find anywhere else. The sites need to be protected and preserved so that future generations can visit and marvel at the wonders of the world.

OXFORD UNIVERSITY PRESS

2 Write words from the text on the previous page in this table. Count the phonemes.

	Word	How many phonemes?
Two-syllable word		
Three-syllable word		
Four-syllable word		

1 There are different ways to spell the **/ear/** phoneme. Say each word. What letter pattern spells the **/ear/** phoneme? Write each word in the correct box.

atmosphere   cheer   hear   interfere   severe

peer   bacteria   career   year   serious   gear

disappear   material   experience   volunteer   sincere

eer	
er	
ere	
ear	

2 Choose three words from the last activity that you don't write very often. Write a definition for each of these words. You may use a dictionary to help you.

Word	Definition

1 Use these charts to help you make words that start with the prefixes **co-** and **pre-**. Add a prefix and a suffix to each base word and write your words in the boxes on the next page. Note, not all suffixes will make words with each base word.

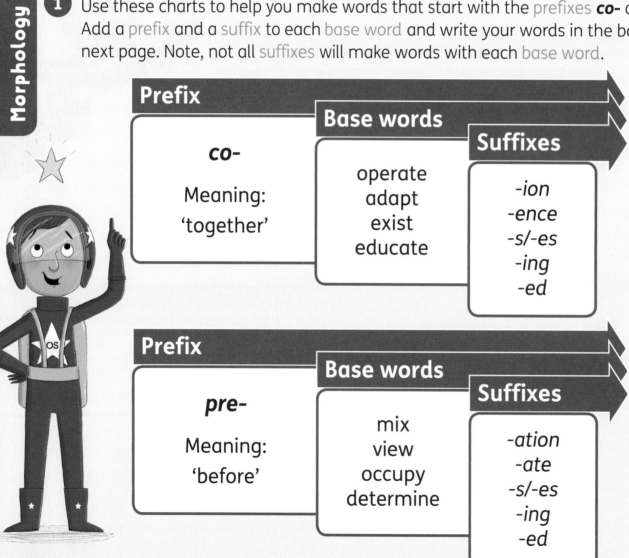

Prefix

co-

Meaning: 'together'

Base words

operate
adapt
exist
educate

Suffixes

-ion
-ence
-s/-es
-ing
-ed

Prefix

pre-

Meaning: 'before'

Base words

mix
view
occupy
determine

Suffixes

-ation
-ate
-s/-es
-ing
-ed

OXFORD UNIVERSITY PRESS

Words starting with the prefix **co-**	Words starting with the prefix **pre-**

2 Choose three words that you wrote in the table above. Write a sentence using each word. Underline the word with the prefix in each sentence.

a _____

_____

b _____

_____

c _____

_____

Now try this unit's 'Bringing it together' activity, which your teacher will give you.

GLOSSARY

adjective	a word that tells us what something is like *small, tall, funny*
alliteration	a group of words starting with the same sound **b**ig **b**lack **b**ears
base word	the smallest part of a word that is also a word on its own *the word 'jump' in 'jumping'*
blend	speech sounds that join together in a word **/st/** *is a blend in the word 'stop'*
consonant	a speech sound made by blocking some air with your lips, teeth or tongue **/b/, /l/, /z/, /v/**
consonant digraph	two letters representing one consonant sound **sh**, **ch**, **th**
contraction	two words joined together with some letters missing. An apostrophe shows us where the missing letters are. *can't (can + not), they're (they + are)*
digraph	two letters representing one phoneme **sh**, **ch**, **oo**, **ee**
diphthong	a kind of long vowel sound that you make by moving your mouth in two ways **/oi/** *in 'boy',* **/ow/** *in 'cow'*
disyllabic word	a word with two syllables *monster (mon-ster), sunshine (sun-shine)*
graph	one letter representing one phoneme **b**, **w**, **o**
homophone	a word that sounds the same as another word but looks different and has a different meaning *eight, ate*
medial	in the middle. A medial phoneme is a speech sound in the middle of a word. This can be a medial vowel or a medial consonant **/o/** *is the medial phoneme in the word 'dog'*
noun	a word that is a name for something, such as a person, place, animal, thing or idea *Ali, school, cat, ball, age*

OXFORD UNIVERSITY PRESS

onset	the sounds in a syllable before the vowel
	b represents the onset in the word 'big'
phoneme	the smallest speech sound you can hear in a word
	the word 'boot' has three phonemes: /b/, long /oo/ and /t/
plural	a word for more than one thing
	'hats' is the plural of the word 'hat'
prefix	letters that go at the beginning of a word to make a new word
	un- in 'unhappy' means 'not' (un- + happy = not happy)
rime	the vowel and other speech sounds at the end of a syllable
	ig represents the rime in the word 'big'
r-influenced vowel phoneme	a vowel that sounds different because it is followed by the letter *r*
	/er/ as in 'mermaid', /air/ as in 'chair'
schwa	an */uh/* sound in a word
	the a in 'balloon' sounds like /uh/
suffix	letters that go at the end of a word to make a new word
	the -s in 'cats' means 'more than one cat'
syllable	a part of a word that feels like a beat and has a vowel sound
	'weekend' has two syllables (week-end)
tense	the way a word is written that shows whether something is in the past, present or future
	'jumped' means the jumping happened in the past
trigraph	three letters representing one phoneme
	igh in the word 'might'
unvoiced phoneme	a sound made using your breath, rather than your voice
	/th/ in 'bath', /s/ in 'salt'
verb	a word for something that happens
	'play' is the verb in the sentence 'I play chess.'
voiced phoneme	a sound made using your voice
	/th/ in 'the', /z/ in 'zoom'
vowel	a sound that you voice with your mouth open and not blocked by your lips, teeth or tongue
	the short /o/ sound in the word 'dog' is a vowel sound

When you have finished the activities in each unit, think about how you feel about the work you have completed.

Draw a ✓ if you feel confident using these ideas on your own.

Draw a ✗ if you feel you need to learn more.

Draw a ◯ if you are not sure.

Unit	Phonology	Orthography	Morphology
1			
2			
3			
4			
5			
6			
7			
8			
9			
10			
11			
12			
13			
14			
15			
16			
17			
18			
19			
20			
21			
22			
23			
24			
25			
26			
27			
28			